The Truth About Olive Oil

Benefits – Curing Methods – Remedies

Joyce Zborower, M.A.

ISBN-10: 1481006266
ISBN-13: 978 1481006262

TABLE OF CONTENTS

FORWARD

By Jim Henry
President Texas Olive Ranch
Executive Director Texas Olive Oil Council

For most of us, olive oil is a mysterious and exotic Italian gourmet item promoted by nutritionists and medical programs. We know it is better than regular cooking oil and that there are some health benefits, but all the reasons why can be murky and confusing to the average person.

When my wife Karen and I visit with our customers we are constantly asked questions like 'what does extra virgin mean?' 'what's so great about olive oil?' 'do you grow green olives or black olives?' 'is it gluten-free?' and 'how long can I keep it before it goes bad?' Sometimes the questions are familiar and sometimes we hear a new one – but what we mostly hear is that people just aren't comfortable with what extra virgin olive oil *is* and *how* to use it and *why* it is good for them, and they don't really trust that what they are buying is what it says it is.

And rightly so. The American olive oil market is a huge and uninformed sector of the world market that has been largely exploited by unscrupulous importers who have taken advantage of America's ignorance for decades — selling their worst quality, adulterated, and fraudulently labeled oils as 'extra virgin' to unsuspecting Americans who just don't know better. Consumer research conducted through the UC Davis Olive Research Center has shown that one third of Americans actually prefer rancid olive oil to fresh because that is what they are familiar with, and they find a flavorful peppery extra virgin off-putting.

Thanks to the courage and dedication of writers like Joyce Zborower and Tom Mueller, more and more Americans are getting the message that extra virgin olive oil has specific qualities and standards that are knowable and desirable, and it's more than just a few words on a label. When someone tastes a fresh extra virgin olive oil from a quality producer, it changes the way they understand olive oil completely. They can taste real olive flavor, experience the delayed sensation of pepperiness that blooms in the back of the throat due to the presence of the compound *oleocanthal* (the same anti-inflammatory found in aspirin), and they realize that it has a fresh, clean mouth feel.

We hear the surprise and amazement over and over again: "Oh, *wow*, that tastes *good!*" Compared to the value-priced imported varieties usually found on grocers' shelves across America, US grown extra virgin olive oil is much fresher, more flavorful, unadulterated, and higher in the polyphenols associated with reduced risk of cancer, diabetes, gastrointestinal and neurological disorders, and more. Extensive research confirms these findings and more health benefits continue to be added as more research is undertaken. It is the *only* food in the highly acclaimed Mediterranean diet that is a single item food group recommended for daily consumption with other foods.

In addition to the health benefits, there are deeply satisfying dimensions of a high quality extra virgin olive oil drizzled on lightly toasted freshly baked bread or roasted vegetables or pasta or risotto that elevate plain and simple food to artisanal levels of experience. Extra virgin olive oil magnifies the essential flavors of the food itself, and intensifies the gustatorial experience even while it contributes to good health and good looks.

Today, American consumers amount to more than 26% of the world olive oil market, and of that we produce less than one percent. That is changing as more and more American farmers in California, Texas, Georgia and Florida plant olive orchards and make more high quality extra virgin olive oil that wins international awards for quality.

In Texas, olives are a new and exciting specialty crop with great potential for growth and economic development — and Texans are particularly proud to know that we grow it and press it *here*. The newly formed American Olive Oil Producers Association is working to improve consumer information about US extra virgin olive oil, and we are optimistic that as the industry grows, more Americans will prefer domestic olive oil to imported.

Karen and I, along with our son and extended family, have spent the last five years personally demonstrating extra virgin olive oils, infused olive oils and balsamic vinegars, and educating folks interested in growing olives and making olive oil. There is enormous interest and passion for this crop and extra virgin olive oil on a domestic, regional and local level.

We invite you to visit our orchard when you are in south Texas. Our harvest is during the weeks of September-October, and we schedule days for public tastings of the brilliantly flavorful freshly pressed '*olio nuovo*' on our website. We hope to see you at one of our farmers markets around the state in the meantime.

Jim Henry

THE TRUTH ABOUT OLIVE OIL

"Olive oil will keep for many years if sealed in a container of glass, steel, or tin – plastic is no good for long storage – and kept in a dark larder. It is best in the first year, and at its healthiest when eaten uncooked, being rich in vitamins A, D, and E, and low in saturated fats, and high in (mono-)unsaturated (fats)."
The Rich Tradition of European Peasant Cooking — ©1987, pp. 496-497.

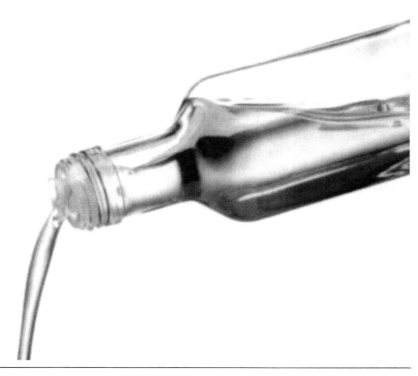

Benefits of Olive Oil

OLIVE OIL: the oldest known monounsaturated fat.
Its beginnings are lost in the clouds of history. Why people ever started to use this bitter fruit and how they found out how to make it edible – let alone palatable — is a mystery. There are many conjectures, yes, but no one really knows for sure. There are surviving records that show the olive's cultivation from as long ago as 6000 years in Syria by a Semitic race for their food value.

— Olives and olive oil have played major roles in the rise and fall of empires.
— Ethnic cuisines are the direct result of the availability of olive oil.
— Folklore and legends abound with stories about olives and olive oil.
— Religions have prized it as holy oil.
— It has been used both internally (as food) and externally (on skin and hair) for health and hygiene. This thought always brings forth in me mental pictures of Roman or Greek bathhouses during the time of Salome where these precious oils were slathered on young supple bodies and then scrapped off with a long instrument.
— Well, everybody else sells sex. Why not? – Olive oil is a lubricant … an edible lubricant.

Enough of that. Back to the more socially acceptable benefits of olive oil.

At various times in its history, olive oil has been used for:

1. – preserving other foods ... this since ancient times and this use has created whole cuisines
2. – medicine ... the leaves can be boiled in water and taken internally or they can be used as an infusion
3. – cooking – especially good for deep fat frying but also useful in various other cooking methods
4. – symbols of peace and prosperity
5. – currency
6. – lamp oil
7. – soap
8.—food in its own right ... olives
9. – fertilizer ... residue from the pressings is spread on the fields
10. – furniture ... the wood of the tree is highly prized and very costly
11. — weapon ... boiled and pored over castle walls onto attacking hordes
12. – the tree's roots bind the soil in erosion-prone lands
13. – olive oil has played and is still playing a prominent role in religious symbolism and ritualism

And, if that's not enough, eating olive oil
14. — helps to reduce LDL cholesterol levels
15. – helps to reduce blood pressure
16. – helps to relieve inflammation and joint pain ... as in arthritis
17. – soothes stomach and intestinal disorders
18. – promotes growth during childhood
19. — may help in weight loss
20. – is extremely digestible by the very old and the very young
21. – extends life expectancy
22. – linked to reduced risk of breast cancer

23. – delays the effects of aging
24. – helps protect against rheumatoid arthritis
25. – contains abundant antioxidants to help protect against free radicals
26. – may help protect against age-related decline in mental functioning
27. – studies show anti-blood clotting effects
28. – populations using olive oil as their main dietary fat enjoy lower rates of both cancer and heart disease than those mainly using other fats

As you can see, there are a ton of very good reasons for making olive oil your primary edible fat – and there's only one main disadvantage. Olive oil provides almost no essential fatty acids. Essential fatty acids are "essential" because these are the substances that the body must get from outside sources as it cannot manufacture them on its own. If you make olive oil your primary dietary fat, you must make sure you are taking in adequate omega-3s from other sources

For keeping olive oil at its best, store it in the refrigerator to protect it from heat, light, air and resulting oxidation/rancidity. Let it sit at room temperature or in warm water to re-liquefy for awhile before using. Buy small quantities and use it up within 2 – 3 months of opening it. Use only cold pressed extra virgin olive oil for whatever you use olive oil for – including cooking, healing and external uses – that is provided in glass containers.

— Every single part of the olive tree is usable by man!

What more could we possibly ask of this lowly little fruit tree?

However, not everyone appreciates this most versatile plant. For example, contrast the above with a prevailing attitude about olive trees held by a number of people in the American southwest. Olive trees are sometimes used as ornamentals here. People complain about allergies to olive pollen and consider the fruit as it falls from the tree to be litter needing to be cleaned up and discarded. The poor maligned olive tree is seen as more of a pest than anything else.

I suspect this opinion is dictated more by a lack of knowledge of how to use the various parts of this tree to their advantage rather than the tree itself. In the pages that follow I hope to stimulate interest in making use of this plant by presenting various "how to do it" scenarios that are practical and fun.

References
Costain, Lyndel, BSc., SRD. *Super Nutrients Handbook – the hidden power in plant foods that can benefit body and mind*. A Dorling Kindersley Book. ©2001.

Ronzio, Robert A., PhD, CNS, FAIC. *The Encyclopedia of Nutrition & Good Health*. Facts on File, Inc. © 1997.

Weil, Andrew, M.D. *Eating Well for Optimum Health – the essential guide to food, diet, and nutrition*. Alfred A. Knopf, NY. © 2000.

Weil, Andrew, M.D. *8 Weeks to Optimum Health – a proven program for taking full advantage of your body's natural healing power*. Alfred A. Knopf, N.Y. © 1997.

Dolamore, Anne. *The Essential Olive Oil Companian – recipes, varieties*. Salem Publications. © 1989.

Knickerbocker, Peggy. *Olive Oil From Tree to Table*. San Francisco: Chronicle Books © 1997.

Shaw, Jerry. *The Healing Power of Olive Oil – learn how it can help you live a longer, healthier life … and look years younger!* (booklet) USA: American Media Mini Mags, Inc. © 2001.

OLEA europaea

Olive Tree Cultivation

The one characteristic of olive trees that endears it to commercial growers is the same characteristic that is the bane of those that consider it to be a pest: ... its ability to grow and thrive in a multitude of conditions. Though they look and do best in deep, rich soil, they also grow well in shallow, alkaline and/or rocky areas with very little fertilizer.

"Both the practical and the mythical popularity of (olive) oil derive, at least partly, from the almost miraculous agronomic characteristics of the olive tree, which thrives even in desert conditions and, when destroyed by fire or frost, sends up green shoots from the root ball through which the tree is reborn." Once established, these trees require very little water. They prefer to live where summers are hot and dry but can also withstand temperatures down to 15° F/-9 C.

Olive foliage is a willow-like soft grey green. Young trees generally have smooth gray trucks that become gnarled and picturesque over time. This aged and gnarled wood is highly prized by woodworkers and so is quite costly.

An evergreen tree that prefers full sun, the olive tree can be found throughout the Mediterranean (Spain, Italy, Greece) which produces ¾ of the world's supply of olive oil as well as in California, Texas, southern Arizona, which produces less than .1% of the world's commercial olive oil, and more recently in Georgia and Florida which will see its first commercial crop since the late 1800s. Commercial varieties include Ascolana, Manzanillo, Mission, Sevillano. There are also several ornamental varieties, some of which produce little to no fruit.

Arbequina, another commercial variety, is said to produce very high quality olive oil and is the recommended variety for commercial production in South Georgia and Florida. They are usually planted with companion plantings of Arbosana and Koroneiki to improve pollination and quality.

According to one agronomist, as reported by Tom Mueller, as olive trees age, their yield "is an upward curve, tending towards infinity."

Since trees sold as 'fruitless' varieties for ornamental plantings are not always barren, care should be taken to gather, remove, and discard fallen fruit as it can stain pavement and harm lawns. The fruit is not edible unless processed. We will discuss how to process the olives for eating later in this book.

Harvesting fruit that is destined for eating or oil production is a time consuming process as it is very important that it is not bruised. Bruising causes the development of acids that detract from the flavor and reduce its grade – and, therefore, the price it will fetch at market which can reach upwards of $3000/barrel for quality organic extra virgin.

The best way to make sure the fruit is not bruised is to hand pick it and this is mostly how olives are harvested. This is time and labor intensive.

If hand picking is not possible, the next best way is to drape a net under the branches and catch the fruit as it falls before it hits the ground. Modified cherry picker machines are also used for harvesting. Some growers refuse to use any olives that have fallen to the ground because of the bruising or other damage sustained by contact with the ground. Others do use them in their lower grade oils.

Green olives are young olives that are not yet ripe. Black olives (ripe olives) are the same olives that have just stayed on the tree long enough to ripen. Olives ripen late in the year.

Pressing the olives tends to be a communal experience in many of the rural areas where there is only one mill for many growers. Waiting their turn at the presses is a time for the men to reconnect with old friends and exchange the latest news of the area. Many times, however, the mill is too far away for that and the fruit is sent to the mill by public transportation with the oil being sent back the same way.

Getting Smaller Quantities Pressed – in U.S.

The commercial growers have made arrangements for getting their crops processed, but what about the non-commercial individuals who have one or just a few trees and would like to get their olives processed? Not to worry. I found two commercial growers who accept smaller loads, combine them, process the olives into cold pressed extra virgin olive oil, bottle it, and return it prorated. Contact information — call to get prices and make your appointment:

Jim Henry
Texas Olive Ranch
6907 Old Preston Place
Dallas, Texas 75252
http://texasoliveranch.com
email: olivehenry@aol.com
214-325-5787

Paul Durant
Red Ridge Farms
Oregon Olive Mill Processing Facility

5510 NE Breyman Orchards Road
Dayton, Oregon 97114
http://redridgefarms.com/oregon-olive-mill
email: paul@redridgefarms.com
503-333-2719

Threats to Olive Production – Olive Fruit Fly

And what about pests? Well, that would be the olive fruit fly, *Bactrocera oleae*. The larvae feed exclusively on olive fruit. Commercial production around the Mediterranean sustains approximately a 30% loss per year due to the damage done by the tunneling larvae. By 1998 this pest had found its way into the California olive groves in Los Angeles and is now found in all areas of California.

Two to five generations of these fruit flies are produced per year throughout the Mediterranean area. In California, adult flies are active throughout the entire year. Insecticides and bait-sprays have been used in both locals to try to control these pests with varying success. Other controls that have been tried include trapping the adults, timing the harvest, sanitizing the fruit after harvest, and biological controls. The latest and most promising control is a wasp (*Psyttalia* cf. *concolor*) from Kenya that acts as a parasite. Hopes are high that this wasp will be able to control and mitigate the damage caused by this fruit fly.

References

Western Garden Book, Sunset Publishing Corp., ©2001. p. 486

http://www.usatoday.com/money/industries/food/story/2011-12-18/olive-oil-farms/51924658/1

http://entnemdept.ufl.edu/creatures/fruit/tropical/olive_fruit_fly.htm

http://qualitygreenspecialists.com/index.php?p=1_13_Fla-Olive-Trees

Mueller, Tom. Extra Virginity – the sublime and scandalous world of olive oil. W.W. Norton & Company: N.Y. © 2012.

What's in a name? that which we call a rose
By any other name would smell as sweet; ...
  William Shakespeare

Olive Oil Classifications

Is It a Description? ... Or Just a Name?

±4000 B.C. – Olive trees were being cultivated in Syria by a Semitic race for their food value. Ancient Palestine was famous for its olive groves and produced fine olive oil which it exported to ancient Egypt.

Olive oil was made in communal vats by peasant women stomping on the olives with their feet – just like grapes as in the making of wine.

±0 some time around the time of Christ 2000 years ago – invention of mechanical presses for making olive oil, wine, etc.

Olive oil today is made in a very similar, though mechanized, way to how it has been made throughout history.

You've heard the term "follow the money"? Well, for the moment, let's consider the nutrients to be the currency of the food. Let's follow the nutrients in olives as they make their journey from the tree to the soap factory – (and/or dinner table).

Olives can be picked in any stage of their development. Black olives are just older, more mature fruits containing more juice (oil) than the younger, harder green olives. Olives are usually picked by hand using the same methods that have been used for centuries.

Once picked, olives that are not to be prepared for table use are quickly brought to the mill to be pressed since leaving them sit in a pile for any length of time results in a higher-acid, lower-quality product. It is to the grower's advantage to bring only the higher quality olives to the mill at one time – and to bring the lower quality olives separately.

Only the finest, unblemished fruit is selected for the first cold press of extra virgin olive oil. Did you know that the juice of the olive – which is what olive oil is – is the only oil that is edible directly from the pressing machine? Every other oil needs to be processed in one way or another to make it usable for human consumption.

"Cold press" is very important for the first pressing of extra virgin olive oil. Heat kills the enzymes. A cold press retains all the nutrient benefits of the raw fruit.

This olive oil directly from the pressing machine, after perhaps being spun to remove the water and filtered to remove any solid particles that remain, is the finest of all the grades produced by that batch of olives. It has been given the name cold pressed extra virgin olive oil and is the oil that we should be using most of the time. Its flavors are said to be as varied as the regions from which it comes. Some are described as "peppery and spicy"; others as "fruity and sweet" – and the descriptions of its colors are exquisite.

As with all other agribusinesses, some growers will opt to use chemical fertilizers and pesticides while others choose to grow their olives organically. If it doesn't say "organic" on the bottle, it isn't, as this is a very good selling point for the oil as well as a way to charge higher prices – and get them.

The nutrient value of freshly cured, whole green olives looks like this:
4 ounces (no pit, in brine): calories, 103; fiber, 2.5g; vitamin E, 2.5mg; rich in flavones luteolin and apigenin, other flavinoids, phenolic acids, and phytosterols. (Costain, Super Nutrients, ©2001, pp. 35, 45.)

At this point, we don't need to know what these things are or what they do in the body. All we need to know is that Nature put them in this food and, if we were to eat these whole cured olives, these things would be a particular nourishment for the body's cells.

Processing and Classifying Olive Oil Grades

At the mill, the olives are crushed, pits and all, which may produce a small amount of heat. The resulting mash is then put into a centrifuge to separate the oil from the natural water that is part of the fruit juice. The oil is then filtered to remove any remaining solid particles. ALL OIL OBTAINED IN THIS MANNER IS CALLED VIRGIN OLIVE OIL. Essentially, the nutrient value of this oil is exactly the same as the nutrient value of the olive. Virgin olive oil (with the exception of Lampante – lamp oil) is fit for human consumption as it is. This is the *only* oil that does not need further refining to make it usable for human consumption. Each batch is then tested and classified into the following Grades:

—— EXTRA VIRGIN OLIVE OIL … has "perfect taste and odour having … maximum acidity of less than 1%." This is the best olive oil you can buy. And this is the *only* olive oil recommended by Dr. Weil. It is also the oil that I am referring to throughout this book.
—— FINE VIRGIN OLIVE OIL … "absolutely perfect taste and odour having … maximum acidity of less than 1.5%."
—— SEMI-FINE OLIVE OIL (ordinary olive oil) … "good taste and odour having … maximum acidity of 3%."
—— VIRGIN OLIVE OIL LAMPANTE (lamp oil) … **not fit for human consumption** "off-taste, off-smelling virgin olive oil with an acidity of more than 3.3 grams per 100 grams. It is intended for refining or for technical purposes." This is the oil that goes to the refinery where it is mixed with water and subjected to high heat and/or chemicals to yield more oil of lesser quality upon each successive pressing. Olive oil obtained by refining is called:

—— REFINED OLIVE OIL ... nutrient value diminished with each pressing. There is little-to-no nourishment (micro-nutrients) in this oil.

What is simply called OLIVE OIL or PURE OLIVE OIL is "oil consisting of a blend of refined olive oil and virgin olive oil." Refined Olive Oil is virtually devoid of nutritional value, flavor, and smell. It's just oil. To give it some semblance of a nutritional product and to make it salable, it <u>must</u> be mixed with virgin oil. Also, it's not generally mixed with the *extra* virgin oil to get some of the benefits of the higher quality oil but with some lesser grade of virgin oil.

At the last pressing, chemicals are added to the mash to extract the last bits of very poor quality oil. This is even a lesser grade of oil called:

—— REFINED OLIVE-RESIDUE OIL ... which is "crude oil obtained by treating olive residues (the remains of Refined Oil pressings) with solvents (chemicals). (It is) intended for subsequent refining for human consumption." There are **no micro-nutrients** in this olive oil. This is "the type (of oil) used largely in the commercial packaging of foods." In other words, for the most part, the commercial food industry is using the poorest quality, cheapest, most nutritionally devoid form of olive oil (and the most likely to contain abundant *trans*-fatty acids) for the foods it provides consumers in the form of "packed in olive oil." There seems to be no attempt to give this form of olive oil even minimal nutritional value by mixing it with some virgin oil.

(This basic information is from "Grades of Olive Oil as Designated by the International Olive Oil Council" as published in: Dolamore, Anne. *The Essential Olive Oil Companion.* Topsfield, Massachusetts: Salem House Publishers. c. 1989. p.37. The conclusions about each grade are mine.)

The above grades are for **real olive oil**. However, according to Tom Mueller in his recent 2012 book, <u>*Extra Virginity – the sublime and scandalous world of olive oil*</u>, fake olive oil ("cheap soybean or canola oil with industrial chlorophyll, dumped in beta-carotene as flavoring, and sold (as) extra virgin") that's dressed up to look like real olive oil readily finds its way onto grocer's shelves. And, apparently, "the U.S. (is) the best place on earth to sell adulterated oil" that looks like it comes from Puglia or Tuscany or Switzerland, etc.

Oil Purity – Is It "Good" or "Bad"

The dictionary definition of "pure" is: 1. Not mixed with anything else; unadulterated; genuine. Free from anything that adulterates, taints, impairs, etc.; unmixed, clear. 2. Perfectly clean; spotless. 3. Without defects; perfect; correct... .

In the context of food, "pure" seems to refer to the removal of the micro-nutrients – the parts of the food that makes it usable and useful in maintaining our health (phytochemicals — enzymes, flavinoids, etc.) – and leaving only the macro-nutrients (protein, carbohydrate, fat) – the calories.

Nothing in Nature is "pure"!

Ordinarily we automatically think of "pure" as a good thing, so when discussing "pure" in relation to things we put in our mouths and swallow, it may be difficult to turn our thinking 180° and realize that, if we need edibles to be as close to Nature as possible, and we do, we don't want "pure".

"Pure" = no health benefits – no enzymes – no phytochemicals – no micro-nutrients. In other words, to borrow a concept from another of my books (**How to Eat Healthy** ... foods to eat – foods to avoid), "pure" = pica, a non-nutritious edible that may change how the cells use food.

Various companies are offering olive oil (Virgin as well as Pure) for sale in plastic bottles. Olive oil has the propensity for 'soaking up' the flavors of things that it comes into contact with; e.g., infusions (flavored oils). In general, plastics have a way of 'giving up' certain of the chemicals that make up their composition to the foods that they come in contact with. Eating oils infused with the chemicals that are given up by the plastics does not sound very appetizing to me. The recommendation is to purchase cold pressed extra virgin olive oil packaged in glass containers only.

References
Costain, Lyndel, BSc, SRD. *Super Nutrients Handbook – the hidden power in plant food that can benefit body and mind*. New York: Dorling Kindersley. © 2001.

Weil, Andrew, M.D. *Eating Well for Optimum Health – the essential guide to food, diet, and nutrition*. Alfred A. Knopf, NY. © 2000.

Weil, Andrew, M.D. *8 Weeks to Optimum Health – a proven program for taking full advantage of your body's natural healing power*. Alfred A. Knopf, N.Y. © 1997.

Dolamore, Anne. *The Essential Olive Oil Companian – recipes, varieties*. Salem Publications. © 1989.

Knickerbocker, Peggy. *Olive Oil From Tree to Table*. San Francisco: Chronicle Books © 1997.

Shaw, Jerry. *The Healing Power of Olive Oil – learn how it can help you live a longer, healthier life ... and look years younger!* (booklet) USA: American Media Mini Mags, Inc. © 2001.

Mueller, Tom. *Extra Virginity – the sublime and scandalous world of olive oil*. W.W. Norton & Co: New York. © 2012.

How to Process Table Olives

Olives right off the tree are hard, bitter and inedible due to a water soluble naturally occurring chemical called *oleuropein*. In processing olive oil, this *oleuropein* is leached out of the olive and into the mash as the olives and their pits are crushed and masticated and is eventually drained and discarded with the water during the centrifuge stage so no other specific step is necessary to remove the bitterness.

Table olives need to be processed in water, brine, dry salt or lye to leach out this chemical, soften the olives, and make them palatable for human consumption. A less often used technique is soaking them in olive oil for several months. This process is called "curing". It's very easy to do but, depending on the process chosen, can take a few weeks to several months before the olives are ready to eat. The chosen process also has a direct effect on the olives' taste and texture.

If possible, processing should begin within two to three days of picking because leaving them longer tends to produce acids within the olives. Brine and dry salt cured olives are saltier than water or lye cured olives. The taste of water cured olives is less changed than with the other curing methods. Lye cured olives tend to be the least flavorful.

Home-cured olives can be stored in brine for varied lengths of time depending on the olive style chosen. Green olives store better than black olives. Storage temperature should be between 41° and 50° for best results. Colder temperatures for longer than two weeks can cause injury to the olives.

CAUTION: If at any time during any of the curing processes the olives become moldy, mushy, or begin to smell bad, discard the entire batch immediately. Do not taste them.

Water Curing – for naturally black ripe olives (cut) or larger green ripe olives (cracked)

Gently wash the olives to remove dirt, leaves and twigs.
Use only unbruised olives.

For black Kalamata-style olives
Use fully-ripe, firm Kalamata or Mission olives – not Sevillano
Cut each olive top to bottom twice with a sharp knife to allow the *oleuropein* to leach out
Place olives in large glass, plastic or ceramic container
Cover with fresh water
Use a large sealed plastic bag filled with water to submerge the fruit
Cover loosely
Change the water after 24 hours
Change the water daily for 8 – 10 days or up to 20 days for less bitter olives
Caution: monitor closely – over-soaking will damage texture and flavor
Drain olives and place in 1 quart or larger glass canning jars
Cover with Finish Brine (see recipe below)
Add 1/4" to 3/8" extra virgin olive oil on top of brine
Seal firmly and store at 60° to 80°F for 1 month to develop flavor before eating
Can be stored for up to 1 year if seal remains air tight

Finish Brine
1 ½ c pickling salt
1 gal. cool water
4 c red wine vinegar

Add salt to water. Stir to dissolve. Add red wine vinegar. Treats ±10# black olives.

For green Mediterranean-style olives
Use any type green-ripe olive for this
Place olive on flat surface – crack skin gently with mallet or rolling pin to allow the *oleuropein* to leach out – do not break or remove pits – do not break apart the olives
Place olives in large glass, plastic or ceramic container
Cover with fresh water
Use a large sealed plastic bag filled with water to submerge the fruit
Cover loosely
Change the water after 24 hours
Change the water daily for 6 - 7 days or a few more days for less bitter olives
Caution: monitor closely – over-soaking will damage texture and flavor
Drain olives and place in 1 quart or larger glass canning jars
Cover with Finish Brine (see recipe below)
Optional – add herbs (oregano, basil, garlic, lemon slices) or other seasonings
Add 1/4" to 3/8" extra virgin olive oil on top of brine
Seal firmly and store at 60° to 80°F for 1 month to develop flavor before eating
Can be stored *in the refrigerator* for up to 1 year if seal remains air tight
Caution: These olives **must** be kept refrigerated.

Finish Brine
1 ½ c pickling salt
1 gal. cool water

2 c white wine vinegar

Add salt to water. Stir to dissolve. Add white wine vinegar. Treats ±10# green olives.

Brine Curing

Curing olives in brine (concentrated salt solution) produces a unique olive flavor as they undergo a natural fermentation process – like sauerkraut or alcohol – as the sugars in the olives break down producing lactic acid and acetic acid. Fermentation does not appreciably alter the nutrient content of the olives which leaves the enzymes intact. There are also some other health benefits to consuming fermented foods – like helping to lower high cholesterol levels in our blood, improving digestion and helping to fight off disease by strengthening our immune system.

According to Nancy Lee Bentley in an article on Dr. Mercola's website titled _The Incredible Benefits to You of Traditionally Fermented Foods_:

"Olives, pickles, grass-fed cheese, wine, yogurt, sauerkraut and the seasoned, aged sausages the French call "charcuterie" are some of this category's most popular delicacies.

Though the term "fermented" sounds vaguely distasteful, the results of this ancient preparation and preservation technique — produced through the breakdown of carbohydrates and proteins by microorganisms such as bacteria, yeasts and molds — are actually delicious. Even more so, **they are so beneficial to overall health that some of these "functional foods" are now considered to be "probiotics,"** increasing your overall nutrition, promoting the growth of friendly intestinal bacteria, and aiding digestion and supporting immune function, including an increase in B vitamins (even Vitamin B12), omega-3 fatty acids, digestive enzymes, lactase and lactic acid, and other immune chemicals that fight off harmful bacteria and even cancer cells."[1]

Curing olives in brine couldn't be simpler. All you need is pickling salt and water along with your choice of olives. The hardest part will be waiting for them to be ready to eat – which could take 3 months or, depending on the variety of olive as well as "temperature, salt concentration, and acidity (pH) of the brine solution", as much as 6 months or longer. Black olives cure faster than green olives. The *oleuropein* (the bitterness in the raw olive) leaches into the brine and is discarded.

Do not alter the brine concentrations given below as the salt acts as a preservative and reduces the possibility for spoilage and ensures consistent fermentation.

Instructions For dark red to purplish black Greek-style olives in brine
Use any variety – Manzanillo, Mission, and Kalamata are most commonly used
To ensure even curing, sort the olives into batches according to size.
Gently wash olives to remove dirt, leaves and twigs.
Use only unbruised olives

Optional — Cutting the olives from top to bottom with a sharp knife helps to release the bitterness.

Pack olives into 1 quart or larger glass Bell™ canning jars

Prepare initial brine (3/4 cup pickling salt per gallon of cool water) and pour over olives

Cover loosely and store at 60° to 80° for 7 days

Drain.

Prepare final brine (1 ½ cups pickling salt per gallon of water) and pour over olives

Cover tightly and store for at least 2 months or, for less bitter taste, replace final brine at 1 month intervals for 2 – 3 months

Check containers regularly and release any built up gas pressure. This is important because excess gas build-up within a closed area could cause the container to explode. Gas is a normal byproduct of fermentation. Reclose tightly.

Can be stored for up to 1 year in a cool, dark place as long as the lids remain tightly sealed and uncorroded.

Refrigerate after opening.

Instructions For green-ripe Sicilian-style olives in brine

Use any variety – Sevillano are most commonly used

Sort according to size

Gently wash olives to remove dirt, leaves and twigs.

Use only unbruised olives

Optional — Cutting the olives from top to bottom with a sharp knife helps to release the bitterness.

Pack olives into 1 quart or larger glass Bell™ canning jars

Add herbs and spices as desired:

    Dill pickle spices – 1T/quart jar of olives — or fresh sprig

    Fennel seed – ½ tsp/quart jar of olives – or fresh sprig

    Chopped garlic

    Whole peppercorns

    Whole dried chili peppers

Brine concentration varies depending on the variety and size of olives

Sevillano and Ascolano – medium solution – 1 cup pickling salt per 1 gal. water

Manzanillo and Mission – strong solution – 1 ½ cups pickling salt per 1 gal. water

Add 2 cups vinegar (5% acidic) to each gallon of brine

Pour brine/vinegar mixture over olives to cover.

Place jars on plastic tray to catch overflow from gas production during fermentation

Loosely close lids.

Store at 70° for 2 months checking jars regularly. Days 1 – 5+, replace brine lost through frothing and foaming. Keep container full of brine at all times.

After 2 months, or when gas stops forming, tighten lids firmly and store for another 2 – 4 months to develop the flavor.

Can be stored in brine for up to 1 year if tightly covered and lids don't corrode.

Dry Salt Curing

Recommended for smaller, hard, fully ripe, unbruised, black, oil rich olives. – Mission commonly used but any small olive with these characteristics will work. Large olives become too soft.

Shorter curing time than other methods – ready to eat in 5 – 6 weeks

Flavor is salty and slightly bitter because less *oleuropein* gets removed with this method

Used for cooking and eating out of hand – to make less salty:
dip into boiling water, let dry, rub with olive oil and herb
mixture before serving

Do this outside.
Place 6" deep wooden or Styrofoam grape crates on a cement
slab that you don't care if it becomes stained or in a large pan
to catch the juices. If placed on the ground, draining salty
juices will kill any vegetation.
These crates should provide drain holes in the bottom and
ventilation on all sides.
Place container on blocks to increase ventilation to bottom
Line entire crate with burlap, cheesecloth, old sheets, cloth
napkins, or something to keep the salt contained and to soak
up any juices expelled from the olives.
Prepare second identical crate.

Lightly wash olives and spread them out to dry
Sort them by size
Discard any bruised or defective olives
Use 1 pound of pickling salt for every 2 pounds of olives
Place olives into container and mix thoroughly with (non-
iodized) pickling salt or kosher salt
Pour another 1 inch of salt over all
Cover with cheesecloth and let stand at 60° to 80°F for 1 week
After 1 week, pour olives into second crate then back into
original crate to re-mix the olives with the salt — (remove any
damaged or rotten olives)
Add a thin layer of new salt over all
Cover with a clean cloth and let stand
Repeat every week for 4 or 5 weeks or until olives are cured
and ready to eat

Pour olives over coarse screening or into a colander to remove excess salt

Spread them out on paper towels or cloth napkins and let dry overnight at room temperature

Optional – dip in boiling water 30 seconds to get rid of excess salt, melt the natural waxy coating on the skin and seal the fruit. Marinate in olive oil for a few days then eat.

To store the cured olives – add 1 ½ cups of salt to each 10 pounds of olives. Mix thoroughly. Pack into 1 quart or larger glass Bell™ canning jars. Cover tightly.

Can be stored up to 1 month (cool, dry place), 6 months (refrigerated) or 1 year (frozen)

Lye Curing of Olives — not covered here.

Most commercial olives are processed with lye.

References

http://articles.mercola.com/sites/articles/archive/2004/01/0
3/fermented-foods-part-two.aspx

http://greekfood.about.com/od/greekcookingtips/qt/cureol
ives.htm

http://www.wikihow.com/Cure-Olives

http://anrcatalog.ucdavis.edu/pdf/8267.pdf

Ronzio, Robert A., PhD, CNS, FAIC. *The Encyclopedia of Nutrition & Good Health*. Facts on File, Inc. © 1997.

A Bowl of Olive Oil

Olive Oil Is 75% Monounsaturated Fat

There are 3 types of natural fat: — saturated fat which is very stable fat from animal products and solid at room temperature – polyunsaturated fat which is much less stable and liquid at room temperature – and monounsaturated fat which is more stable than 'poly' and also liquid at room temperature. (Hydrogenation is the man-made process of stabilizing unsaturated fats – primarily polyunsaturates.

It produces unnatural saturated fats that are damaging to humans. It is recommended that we avoid eating hydrogenated or partially hydrogenated fats.)

Monounsaturated fat is "the good fat" ... the kind you should be eating more of. Olive oil contains more monounsaturated fat than any other edible oil (see fig. 1). And olive oil is the only oil that does not require any treatments other than cold pressing to be palatable and fit for human consumption.

OIL or FAT	% Monounsaturated Fatty Acids
Olive Oil	75%
Canola Oil	58%
Safflower Oil	12%
Corn Oil	24%
Coconut Oil	6%
Flaxseed Oil	18%
Sunflower Oil	20%
Soft Tub Margarine ***	47%
Stick Margarine ***	59%
Soybean Oil	23%
Peanut Oil	46%
Cottonseed Oil	18%
Vegetable Shortening ***	51%
Chicken Fat	45%
Lard (pork fat)	45%
Beef Tallow	42%
Palm Oil	37%
Butter	29%
Tuna Fat ****	26%
Palm Kernel Oil	11%
Avocado Oil	69%
Almond Oil	68%

Figure 1 — % Monounsaturated Fatty Acids in Edible Oils and Fats
*** made with hydrogenated soybean oil + hydrogenated cottonseed oil
**** fat from white tuna, canned in water, drained solids
http://www.nutristrategy.com/fatsoils.htm

As you can see by the chart above, monounsaturated fatty acids (MUFAs) are found in both plant and animal products. It's called the good fat because it tends to lower LDL cholesterol levels (the so-called "bad" cholesterol — though both "good" (HDL) and "bad" (LDL) cholesterol are necessary for the body to function properly) while not lowering, but slightly increasing, the HDL cholesterol in healthy people and those with inherited cardiovascular diseases. Polyunsaturated fatty acids (PUFAs), in contrast, — while still needed in our diet for the essential fatty acids they provide — tend to lower both LDL and HDL.

Here are the other main benefits of eating monounsaturated fats:

➢ Recommended for cooking as they are safer and healthier
➢ When heated, they produce fewer free radicals than other oils
➢ They resist rancidity
➢ MUFAs contained in our body fat can be burned as energy

Why Lowering LDL Cholesterol is a Good Thing

"Elevated LDL is considered to be an approximate or rough index of cardiovascular risk among U.S. men."

LDL is a lipid-protein particle that transports cholesterol from the liver to other tissues via the bloodstream. LDL carries 60 to 80% of the cholesterol found in the serum (the clear fluid remaining after blood has clotted and blood cells are removed). LDL absorbs and dissolves cholesterol. Docking sites on target cells possess a unique protein called apolipoprotein B. These cells absorb the LDL then destroy it and the cholesterol is either incorporated into the cell membranes or it is stored. Interfering with this process increases the risk for atherosclerosis, i.e. plaque build-up in arteries.

The target LDL-cholesterol level is less than 130 mg/dl in healthy men and 100 mg/dl or less for those with heart disease. 130 – 150 mg/dl is considered borderline high.

HDL performs the opposite function. It transports cholesterol from the tissues (muscles) back to the liver for disposal. Specific laboratory tests can assess the relative LDL/HDL ratios. A lower LDL and higher HDL level are desirable because this ratio reduces the risk of stroke or heart attack. "HDL cholesterol should be greater than 35 for men (50 for women) and values greater than 65 can protect against diseased arteries."

What is the Function of Free Radicals in the Body and Why it's Better to Have Fewer of Them

Free radicals are "highly reactive molecules that can initiate chain reactions of chemical disruption, injuring cell membranes, enzymes, and DNA itself."

What that means in English is that free radicals contain molecules of oxygen that are readily available for combining with atoms that are missing hydrogen components in their makeup. For example, polyunsaturated oil is missing many hydrogen components in its chemical formula and is therefore eager to acquire components that will fill the empty places. It greedily latches onto the free radical's oxygen molecules. This oxygenation of the oil spoils the oil which makes it smell bad and taste bad. This oxygenated oil is said to be rancid (decomposed) and is no longer edible because rancidity produces *trans*-fatty acids, TFAs. (see below).

High consumption of polyunsaturates is more likely to promote the oxidation of LDL cholesterol … thus increasing the probability that oxidized LDL will be taken up by the blood vessels and create plaque in the arteries." Also, according to certain animal studies, polyunsaturates tend to increase the risk for some forms of cancer. It is recommended that cooking be done with olive oil as opposed to other oils because olive oil is more stable when heated – therefore safer and healthier. (Stable means that olive oil is less likely to produce free radicals when heated.)

What Causes Oils/Fats to Become Rancid

Unsaturated fats are liquid at room temperature making them more vulnerable to attack by oxygen – which can lead to rancidity (decomposition). In contrast, saturated fats are solid at room temperature and are more stable to heat and oxidation.

Oxidation causes oils and fats to become rancid ... but what is oxidation? To understand this, we need to look at the chemical composition of the oil.

There are two types of unsaturated fats: monounsaturated and polyunsaturated. Saturated fats have all their carbon atoms attached to hydrogen atoms. They are stable in that there is no room for oxygen atoms to attach themselves. Monounsaturated fats are missing one set of hydrogen atoms for all their carbon atoms and polyunsaturated fats are missing many hydrogen atoms therefore providing many possible attachment sites for oxygen atoms. Rancidity occurs as oxygen atoms attach to carbon atoms in place of hydrogen atoms and is promoted by heat and light and air.

Why We Should NOT Eat Rancid Oils/Fats

Rancid oils smell rank and taste stale, not fresh, spoiled. "When oxidation reacts with unsaturated fatty acids, the result is the formation of a range of dangerous compounds …
If you are unsure what rancid fat smells like, just sniff linseed oil or oil paint, and if you detect anything similar in nuts, chips, flour, or baked goods you are tempted to eat, throw them out at once. Oxidized oils promote arterial damage, cancer, inflammation, degenerative disease, and premature aging of cells and tissues."

TFAs – Trans-fatty Acids

For those not familiar with *trans*-fatty acids, *trans*-fatty acids, or TFAs, are unnatural forms of unsaturated fatty acids. "The body uses *cis* forms of fatty acids to build membranes and hormones; given *trans* forms to work with, it might produce defective membranes and defective hormones." Weil, *Eating Well* … p. 91. *Trans*-fatty acids are what make fats taste and smell rancid. Rancid smelling fats should never be eaten. They are formed through processing but can also form after extraction through exposure to light and heat and air. For this reason, olive oil should be kept under air tight seal in a cool, dark environment. Purchasing small quantities and using it up quickly (within 2-3 months of opening it) is probably a wise idea.

How Does Our Body's Burning MUFAs Benefit Us

"All fats and oils are mostly mixtures of different triglycerides. When we eat them, the body frees the fatty acids from their glycerol carriers and rearranges them into new triglycerides for its own uses. Stored triglycerides in the body's fatty (adipose) tissue are primarily reserves of calories; so to get to those calories the body again separates the fatty acids (primarily SFAs and MUFAs) from glycerol and sends them to sites of cellular oxidation, where they are burned for energy." And this is how olive oil helps in weight loss.

To help with their weight loss or weight maintenance goals, some folks swallow a tablespoonful (or two) of olive oil in the mornings right from the bottle. If your body is not used to this, the olive oil can function as a laxative.

Take-Aways Regarding Olive Oil

> Heat and light and exposure to air promote rancidity in oils. This is why olive oil is often sold in dark green bottles as this shields the oil from light. At home, store your olive oil in a cool, dark place like in the refrigerator (or covered on your kitchen counter away from the stove).

- ➢ Olive oil does not get better with age. Buy oil in small quantities and use it up within 2 – 3 months of opening.
- ➢ If you're going to cook with oil, use olive oil because olive oil does not break down into TFAs (*trans*-fatty acids) as readily as other oils which makes it a safer and healthier oil to cook with.
- ➢ Since olive oil consists of ±75% monounsaturated fats, eating olive oil consistently will raise your HDL cholesterol and help protect you from heart attack and stroke.
- ➢ Our bodies can burn the monounsaturated fatty acids for energy which is why olive oil helps in weight loss.
- ➢ Since cold pressed extra virgin olive oil does not require further processing to be palatable and edible, the nutrients that were in the fresh fruit are still present in the oil, therefore olive oil is more nutritious and better for your health than any of the other oils.

References

http://www.nutristrategy.com/fatsoils.htm

Ronzio, Robert A., PhD, CNS, FAIC. *The Encyclopedia of Nutrition & Good Health*. Facts on File, Inc. © 1997.

Weil, Andrew, M.D. *Eating Well for Optimum Health – the essential guide to food, diet, and nutrition*. Alfred A. Knopf, NY. © 2000.

Infusions and Dipping Oils

Olive oil has the ability to absorb the flavors and aromas of whatever it comes in contact with. "The primary lipid component of oil, oleic acid, is a powerful solvent which also enables oil to extract flavors in cooking and hold fragrances in perfume." This presents some very interesting culinary possibilities in the form of infused oils. Using infused oil on vegetables or meat can add savory additions to otherwise ordinary dishes. They can also be used in salad dressings, marinades, and sauces.

Infusions are very easy to make. Just combine herbs and/or spices with oil and let it sit for a couple of weeks for the olive oil and the aromatic oils in the herbs/spices to combine. Or, for a quicker method, the mixture can be heated – slowly so it doesn't burn. Olive oil infusions will remain usable for about a month if stored in the refrigerator.

Caution: The oil by itself will not support bacterial growth. However, using fresh herbs/spices such as garlic, japaleño, parsley, etc. in an infusion could provide a beneficial environment for bacterial growth because of the water in the fresh vegetation. Botulism bacteria could be produced in this type of environment. As you know, botulism can make you very ill. If you prefer to use fresh herbs/spices, store the flavored oil in the refrigerator and use it up within 1 week.

Infusions

Use 4 to 4½ cups oil to 1 cup dried herb or spice.

To make herb infusions, use 1 cup of whole, dried leaves. Some possibilities are tarragon, rosemary, basil, mint, chives, oregano, dill, etc.

To make spice infusions, use either dried whole or ground spices such as cardamom, cinnamon, cumin, cloves, anise, etc. If heating the mixture and using ground spices, strain the mixture through cheesecloth before bottling it.

You could also choose one herb and one spice for a different kind of taste.

Healing Properties of Herbs and Spices

In addition to flavoring various dishes, olive oil infusions can also have medicinal properties that have long been used as home remedies for various ailments. The healing properties of various herbs and spices have been known and used since before biblical times and they are no less effective today. And when these healers are combined with the innate healing powers of olive oil, you have a powerful combination for healing right from your kitchen cabinets. Just remember that all of the following are based on anecdotal evidence – not scientific fact.

This is not an exhaustive list – just a sampling that is paraphrased from Cal Orey's book:

GARLIC has long been used as a healing food. It has anti-inflammatory properties that make it particularly useful in poultices. It is also used as a diuretic and sedative. Some internal parasites thrive on a diet of oleic acid (olive oil), so when used to kill parasites do not use the infusion.

JAPALENO peppers are rich in the anti-oxidants A, C, and E. Hot jalapeno peppers are great for clearing your sinuses because of its capsaicin – that's what makes it hot. It also helps to slow down cancer cell growth and relieves migraine pain. Anti-inflammatory properties are also prevalent.

OREGANO oil, another anti-inflammatory, helps fight cold and flu viruses as well as killing bacteria, fungi and other germs.

PARSLEY is a cleansing herb. It has anti-oxidant vitamins A, C, and E along with a good bit of iron. Parsley is used as a diuretic and also is said to relieve PMS symptoms: cramps, mood swings, and bloating.

ROSEMARY is an ancient therapeutic herb that's used to cure headaches, hemorrhoids, and depression, etc. It's also good for balancing the fluids around the nerves and heart.

SAGE is a natural astringent and antiseptic that is used against gum disease and sore throats.

THYME is also an antiseptic and general healing tonic that's used to stop coughing and relieve intestinal disorders.

Glass vs. Plastic Containers

I said this once earlier in this book but it's important … so I'll say it again here. We've just been talking about the propensity of olive oil to absorb the flavors and aromas of whatever it comes into contact with. In many instances this is a good thing. It allows us to have different oils for different uses and increases the ways in which we can use olive oil to benefit us.

However, some manufacturers are packaging olive oil in plastic containers for distribution to consumers. Plastic containers are good and useful for many things – but not for olive oil. Plastic gives up certain of its chemicals; olive oil, when in contact with this plastic, will absorb these chemicals which may affect its taste and smell. Personally, I don't want to eat the chemicals in plastics. I recommend that we purchase only cold pressed extra virgin olive oil packaged in glass containers.

Dipping Oil

My first introduction to really great dipping olive oil was about 30 years ago. My husband and I went to a delightful Mediterranean restaurant. That restaurant is still there, by the way. We knew nothing about Mediterranean food or healthy eating or olive oil, for that matter.

The owner was very kind … Very helpful and friendly. We let him choose the foods for our meal. I have vivid memories of sopping up delicious oil with chunks of fresh baked bread and relishing every morsel. The rest of the meal was also fantastic. Smells. Tastes. Textures.

But I was worried about gaining weight from eating all that fat. As much as I loved the food, I believed the "dieting logic" of the time (which is not so different from the "dieting logic" of today – 2012) and didn't allow myself those pleasures again for many years.

I hope you don't deny yourself the pleasures of olive oil because of someone else's misguided and misunderstood notions about what is or is not good for your body.

Olive oil is good for you. Take a look at the first chapter again and you'll see the many, many ways in which your body benefits from your use – internally as well as externally – of this historically highly prized and precious liquid.

Prepared infused and/or dipping oils can be purchased from:
Texas Olive Ranch
online store: **www.texasoliveranch.com**
email: **store@texasoliveranch.com**
phone: 855.TX.OLIVE **(855.896.5483)**

References

http://www.exploratorium.edu/cooking/seasoning/kitchen/recipe-oils.html

Orey, Cal. *The Healing Powers of Olive Oil – a complete guide to nature's liquid gold*. Kensington Books. © 2000.

Olive Oil Massage Relieves Aches and Pains

Olive Oil as Folk Remedy

Real extra virgin olive oil, by itself, has remarkable healing properties – both internally and externally. "The powerful anti-oxidants and anti-inflammatories … help to prevent degenerative conditions – like … cancer." Certain supermarket varieties may not provide such powerful healing properties and if you're going to use olive oil for healing, as opposed to simply flavoring dishes, make sure you purchase *real* cold pressed extra virgin olive oil, preferably from the processor.

I remember reading somewhere that the beautiful Sophia Loren used to bathe in olive oil. It's a great story but I don't know if that's true. Her skin was lovely, though. And it's not unusual for people to rub olive oil all over their body — hands, feet, hair, belly – it's even soothing for a chafed crotch. They even feed it to their pets and rub it on their coats to get rid of tics. As with the healing properties of herbs and spices, the following sampling of the healing effects of olive oil is offered based on anecdotal evidence, not scientific fact.

Tom Mueller writes beautifully about the properties of this "slippery, subtly mysterious substance, a vegetable oil made from a fruit, a fresh fruit juice with the ideal blend of fats for the human body, a fat that slims the arteries and nourishes the mind, an age-old food with space-age qualities that medical science is just beginning to understand.

… Oil obsession is an ancient condition. Rereading poems and sacred texts I thought I knew well, I caught glints and scents I'd never noticed before, of a time when olive oil was not only an essential food, but a catalyst of civilized life and a vital link between people and the divine. Odysseus, haggard and salt-crusted after a shipwreck, spreads his body with oil and suddenly appears as handsome as a god. Mary Magdalene, the repentant prostitute, anoints Christ's feet with an aromatic oil that fills the house with its fragrance, then wipes them clean with her hair. The Prophet Mohammed, peace be upon him, uses so much oil on his skin that his shawl is often drenched with it … The fruit and fragrance are tempered with bitterness, as life's beauty is."

He goes on: "I tried olive oil as a skin lotion: it softened chapped lips and soothed sunburn and healed my baby daughter's diaper rash with one application. I made a batch of soap on the stovetop ... pouring the resulting paste into molds I'd cut from blocks of olive wood. The soap produced a pinkish, faintly slimy lather which left the skin wonderfully soft ... I tested olive oil's qualities as a solvent and lubricant, polishing mirrored surfaces on an old toaster and chrome trim, revealing new depths of grain in a battered walnut tabletop, silencing squeaky windows throughout the house. I poured out little jars of oil and dropped in garlic cloves, rosemary sprigs, orange rind, and boiled eggs, and found within days that their olfactory essences had leached into the oil and now lingered there, magically imprisoned, like genies in a bottle. I jury-rigged a still from a pressure cooker and a coil of copper tubing, used it to extract essential oils from lavender, wisteria, jasmine, and bergamot, then stirred these essences into an olive oil base, creating vividly scented oils which I rubbed on my face, and furtively into my hair, thinking how it would be to play the Old Testament priest and pour the entire jar over my head, drenching my beard and dripping from my clothes."

Doesn't he paint beautiful word-pictures? ... while, at the same time, giving us a myriad of practical uses for a wonderfully beneficial substance.

Cal Orey provides us with a number of other potentially equally useful treatments. She lists 30. I'll paraphrase a few of them here:

BLADDER INFECTIONS, a burning pain during urination: mix 1 teaspoon of olive oil with one teaspoon of garlic juice. Drink 3 times per day, preferably before meals. Drink 100% cranberry juice as a preventive measure (sold in health food stores – not the same as cranberry juice cocktail).

SKIN BURNS from cooking or drinking a beverage that's too hot have been successfully treated by applying extra virgin olive oil three or four time a day. Olive oil has an anti-biotic effect and is soothing. For burns to your mouth or lips, olive oil is gentle and edible.

COUGHING or a tickle in your throat can be can calmed by "taking 1 tablespoon of olive oil as needed."

CONSTIPATION? Forget about cod liver oil. It doesn't taste good … but olive oil does and its laxative powers are well known. Eat plenty of fruits and veggies and take 1 or 2 tablespoons of olive oil and drink plenty of water.

MILD EARACHES, such as from swimmer's ear, can be cured and the pain healed with a few drops of warmed (not hot) olive oil placed into the ear canal. Repeat as needed.

DIAPER RASH or CHAFED CROTCH or SUNBURN can be treated by shaking together 2 teaspoons of olive oil with 1 teaspoon water until you get a creamy, pasty emulsion that can be spread on the skin. It's soothing, anti-bacterial action helps you feel better quickly.

GINGIVITIS is puffy, bloody gums. Use the same emulsion as for diaper rash, but rinse your mouth with it. This remedy also decreases plaque formation.

HOT FLASHES are the bane of many a woman during menopause. To lessen their severity, drizzle 1 tablespoon of olive oil onto 5 servings of veggies per day. Use all kinds of vegetables.

MUSCLE ACHES can be lessened by using warmed olive oil applied as a massage oil.

PSORIASIS can be a painful skin condition that may be helped with the application of olive oil. Massage it generously into the affected areas at bedtime. Rinse it off in the morning. Repeat as necessary.

Olive oil has been used as a SEXUAL LUBRICANT for centuries, either with a partner (as it is an edible oil and also helps vanquish vaginal dryness that can cause pain during intercourse) or for self-pleasuring for males.

Here you have 12 highlights of Orey's 30 olive oil treatments. Her book is available at libraries or book stores if you'd like to check out the rest of them.

References
Orey, Cal. *The Healing Powers of Olive Oil – a complete guide to nature's liquid gold*. Kensington Books. © 2000.

Mueller, Tom. *Extra Virginity – the sublime and scandalous world of olive oil*. W.W. Norton & Co: New York. © 2012.

DISCLAIMER

This book is presented solely for informational and educational purposes so you can learn more about the subject.

The information provided in **The Truth About Olive Oil** is NOT INTENDED TO PROVIDE MEDICAL ADVICE OR TREAT OR CURE ANY DISEASE OR HEALTH PROBLEM OR OFFER ANY SPECIFIC DIAGNOSIS TO ANY INDIVIDUAL. You should always consult your licensed healthcare professional before making significant changes to your diet or taking any form of medication.

I am NOT a licensed healthcare professional. My background and degrees are in Clinical Psychology and Certified Professional Coaching. However, I have had college level training in biology, human physiology and nutrition and have done extensive independent research in nutrition.

While I have made significant effort to provide accurate information, the information provided here should NOT be considered complete and exhaustive of the topic and I DISCLAIM ANY LIABILITY OR LOSS IN CONNECTION WITH YOUR USE OF THE INFORMATION CONTAINED HEREIN. YOUR USE OF ANY INFORMATION PROVIDED HERE IS TOTALLY YOUR RESPONSIBILITY.

You should never disregard medical advice or delay in seeking it because of something you have read here. This information is not intended as and should not be used in place of a visit to or consultation with or the advice of a physician or other qualified health care provider.

Books by Joyce Zborower

Link to my Amazon page: **http://amzn.to/MIKKpJ**
The Trust– a cautionary tale
Little Mysteries – a short story
Handcrafted Jewelry Step by Step – beginner and intermediate original designs
Handcrafted Jewelry Photo Gallery – cast jewelry — fabricated jewelry
Wire Jewelry Photo Gallery– Original Designs
Creations in Wood Photo Gallery – jewelry boxes, screens, storage ideas
Bargello Quilts Photo Gallery– quilt wall hangings
Bargello Train Quilt – cutting and sewing instructions
Sell Your Work – how to turn your craft into your business
Psychology of Success – how to have success when trying to change how you look
No Work Vegetable Gardening – for in-ground, raised beds, or container gardening
How To Eat Healthy – foods to eat …foods to avoid
The Truth About Olive Oil – benefits, curing methods, remedies

Paperback Books
Little Mysteries – a short story
Sell Your Work – how to turn your craft into your business
No Work Vegetable Gardening – for in-ground, raised beds, or container gardening
The Truth About Olive Oil – benefits, curing methods, remedies

Español Libros (Spanish language Books) –

Available or Coming Soon

Mi página de Amazon **http://amzn.to/MIKKpJ**
El Fideicomiso – fábula con moraleja
Pequeños Misterios– cuento
Joyas Hechas a Mano Paso a Paso – diseños originales para nivel principiantes e intermedio
Joyas Hechas a Mano Galería de fotos – joyería fundida—joyería manufacturada
Joyas de Alambre Galería de fotos – Diseños originales
Creaciones en Madera Galería de fotos – joyeros, biombos, ideas de almacenaje
Quilts Estilo Bargello Galería de fotos ta– pices de quilt
Quilt Tren en Bargello– instrucciones para cortar y coser
Venda suTrabajo – como transformar tu arte en negocio
La Psicología del Éxito – cómo tener éxito al tratar de cambiar tu apariencia
Huerto sin Esfuerzo – para jardinería en el suelo, elevada o en contenedor
Como Comer Sano – comidas para comer…comidas para evitar
La Verdad Acerca del Aceite de Oliva– beneficios, métodos de curación, remedios

Other Recommended Books

CHARACTER – a 45 year romp through the working life of an emergency mental health professional — — by John F. Walsh, M.S.

Character is the sometimes funny, sometimes poignant remembrances of a psychologist/counselor of the characters (both staff and patients) who peopled his 45 years as a mental health professional — primarily dealing with emergency issues within a mental health facility. And along the way, we discover a thing or twenty about how people think and about how the way they think has a tremendous impact on how they behave.

The Confession of a Trust Magnate — —- by George Allen Yuille
*Picture the combined navies of the world
anchored off our seaboard cities, the
combined armies of the world in possession
of our inland cities, envoys from each
nation congregated at Washington
partitioning our country, the entire population
being apportioned as slaves to do the bidding
of the conquerors.*
Would you be interested?
*An equally appalling situation confronts
the people of this country to-day.*
Read of it in the pages of this book.

The Confession of a Trust Magnate was written in 1911. Its message is critical for today – 2012.

Questions & Comments

I'd love to hear your thoughts.
Email me at **admin@hunting4clients.com**

Need help?

Are you an aspiring writer who's having trouble getting your book published? My company does book editing and formatting and posts client's books to Create Space, Smashwords, and KDP.

My GURANTEE: Your book will pass the Smashwords' Meat-grinder and Auto-vetter and/or the formatting requirements of Create Space and/or KDP or you pay nothing.
You can reach me at **admin@hunting4clients.com**

One Last Thing Before You Go...

If you believe the book is worth sharing, would you take a few seconds and let your friends know about it at Facebook and Twitter? If it turns out to make a difference in their lives, they'll be forever grateful to you. As will I.

All the best
Joyce Zborower

or ... go to my Amazon page: **http://amzn.to/MIKKpJ**
Click the book cover to get to the 'Review This Book' button and let your opinion influence others.

CPSIA information can be obtained at www.ICGtesting.com
Printed in the USA
LVOW05s2305050314

376166LV00028B/1205/P